Sales Surge:
50 Secrets to Propel Your Sales Career With Less Stress and More Fun!

By Henry Oliver

Text copyright © 2019 Henry Oliver
All Rights Reserved

No part of this book may be reproduced in any form or by any means – electronic, mechanical, photo copy, recording, scanning, or other - without permission in writing from the author.
This material is designed to provide educational information regarding the subject matter covered. However, the author and publisher are not offering any professional service or professional advice, including in the areas of sales, accounting, financial, legal or other areas. Please consult a professional for expert advice if service in any of these areas is needed.
No warranty is made with respect to the accuracy, validity or completeness of the content provided. The author, publisher and their assigns specifically disclaim any responsibility for any liability, loss or risk occurred as a consequence, directly or indirectly from the use and application of any information contained in this publication. This publication is designed for educational and entertainment purposes only. Please consult a professional in your area for any specific advice or application. The views expressed in this book do not represent any organization, institution or association. They are strictly the views of the author, and are meant for education and entertainment purposes only.
The author and publisher are not responsible for any third party websites or hyperlinks contained within this material. The author and publisher are not responsible for viruses, malware or other computer scripts or damage that may occur from third party websites or links. Readers who click on hyperlinks do so at their own risk.

The two books in this Sales Surge series by Henry Oliver

Available at Amazon and Audible

Sales Surge: 50 Secrets to Propel Your Sales Career With Less Stress and More Fun!

Sales Surge Sequel: Another 50 Secrets to Boost Your Sales Career With Less Stress and More Fun!

For more bonus information about the awesome books, influential thought leaders and helpful links we refer to in the book, please visit:

SaleSurgeBook.com

Dedication

For sales professionals everywhere, who wake up every day striving for self-improvement. By going the extra mile and serving our customers to the best of our ability, we build prosperous careers and make a real difference in the world around us.

Table of Contents

Introduction	10
1 Put the customer first.	13
2 Pressure wins now.	15
3 It is all about the numbers.	17
4 Your customer doesn't get it.	19
5 Fill your brain with the good stuff.	20
6 Is a phone follow-up just as effective as an in-person visit?	21
7 Cure your aversion to cold calling.	23
8 Consistency is key.	25
9 Kill the frog every day.	27
10 Get to know Brian Tracy.	28
11 How many referrals have you collected today?	30
12 Busy does not equal successful.	31
13 Send the article.	32
14 Send the note.	33
15 Drop by.	34
16 What are your top five objections?	36
17 What did you learn about your industry today?	38

18 Tops in sales does not necessarily equal tops in management. 39

19 Align with the company culture. 40

20 Organize your bag. 41

21 Set boundaries on your time. 42

22 The customer is always right. 43

23 Get to know Zig Ziglar. 44

24 In ten seconds, what do you sell? 45

25 Set one, three and five-year goals. 46

26 What podcasts have you listened to today? 47

27 Get to know Earl Nightingale. 48

28 Executives are busy. 49

29 What happens two minutes after you leave? 50

30 What is your brand? 51

31 Do you make the team better? 52

32 Don't gamble on your future. 53

33 The industry and you. 54

34 (First-rate) recruiters can be your ally. 55

35 Don't neglect your family. 57

36 Video vs text. 58

37 Don't bad-mouth the competition.	59
38 Dress as if you were a professional.	60
39 Identify the culture of the customer.	61
40 Objections are not personal.	62
41 Know your "WHY."	63
42 Know your customer's "WHY."	64
43 Track expenses.	65
44 Manage the adrenaline.	66
45 Attack today while thinking long-term.	67
46 A sale today is not worth damaging your reputation.	68
47 Get to know Napoleon Hill.	70
48 The supermarket duck-away.	71
49 Don't be cute with your customer.	73
50 With multiple products, what is most important to the customer?	74
The next step...	76

Introduction

Why do some sales professionals launch to seemingly instant success, while others languish for months, years or decades?

Why does it seem to come so naturally for some salespeople, while many continue to work - day in and day out - for small and fleeting results?

Why do some sales pros build a long-term career free of stress and full of prosperity, personal growth and fulfilling relationships?

Are there secrets that sales winners understand and put into action that others do not?

This book will pull back the curtain on the real world of professional sales, so you can reach toward the success you've been dreaming of. There are no guaranteed results, and this book won't be a magic wand to instantly transform your career from mediocre to off-the-charts awesome. But what it will do is help you improve and make you better than you are today.

In the pages that follow, you'll realize that you may already be incorporating many of these 50 secrets into your daily sales activities. Awesome, give yourself a pat on the back! Perhaps many more of the "secrets" are techniques you can put into effect today to help you improve and grow.

The truth is...they aren't secrets at all.
These are proven success principles and tips that have been used and taught by successful sales professionals for centuries. In fact, we'll highlight and link to other thought leaders, books and resources that can help you continue your journey toward higher levels of sales success. This is the beginning of a journey that never ends.

You deserve a sales career that takes off and surges to higher levels.

You deserve a career with less stress and much more fun and enjoyment.
So let's get started!

1 Put the customer first.

The customer is the one and only reason you are a sales professional at all. He is your reason for existing. Regardless of your knowledge, skill, business acumen or world-changing product, you are nothing without a customer. There are two sides to the equation - supply and demand. You have the supply and the customer provides the demand. While a willing buyer cannot move forward without you and your killer widget, a prepared and practiced sales professional cannot advance his career, or sell his wares, without a customer to serve. After establishing this irrefutable truth and placing the customer in his proper place of honor, how, then, should we treat this customer? After all, there is not success or advancement in our business without him. The answer should be simple. We treat the customer as though he comes first or, rather, his NEEDS come first. We are in existence to serve the customer. To the extent we can do that, with quality and frequency, we determine the height of our sales success. It is all about putting the customer first.

2 Pressure wins now.

Consultation wins in the long term. Have you read any of the myriad of sales books touting tricks and methods of pressuring a customer into a sale? Some books are filled with entire chapters of "closing techniques." While many of these are terrific and extremely valuable (see Tip #10 regarding Brian Tracy), approaches based on pressure should be looked at with a jaundiced eye. Pressure may get you the sale today, or it may not. However, that pressure-induced sale may change the way the customer feels about you. In the long run, this feeling is what helps build the long-term relationship and keep the sales coming for many months or years. This long-term growth is exactly how to build a winning, lasting sales career. If you treat someone well today, through a consultative, customer-centered approach, he will see you as a member of his team. He will trust you and rely on you the next time he's in the market for your type of product. You will see his number pop up on your phone when he needs to re-order. Do customers call back if they felt pressured the first time? Rarely. This doesn't mean you don't close the sale and move the process to completion. It simply means doing so in a balanced, consultative manner. What about if your business entails a relatively quick, one-time transactional sale? For example, you sell a single product only one time to each customer. Will a low-pressure approach lead to your best long-term gains? The answer is the same - YES! The reason is that, even in a one-time transactional sale, the customer is often in a position to provide you with referrals - warm leads that are ready, willing and able to buy from you. By turning down the pressure in your approach, you increase the odds you'll get both quality and quantity of referrals from each completed sale. Consult with your clients, rather than pressuring them. You will both appreciate that approach.

3 It is all about the numbers.

Sales is a numbers game. Whether you sell cars, houses, medical devices, books or paper clips, the more qualified prospects you talk to, the more of your product or service you will sell. In other words, the more calls you make on people who need and are in the market for what you sell, the more of it you WILL sell. If you visit ten restaurants trying to sell ketchup, you'll most likely sell less than if you visit 100. (I've never sold ketchup but I should, seeing how much my girls and I gobble up in my house.) After a while selling in a particular industry, you can basically calculate how many prospects you need to present your solution to in order to reach your sales goal. And by prospect, I mean someone who can reasonably be expected to be in the market for what you sell.

For example, if I know I can sell my wrenches to three out of every ten mechanics I present them to, I'd reasonably expect to sell 15 wrenches if I present them to 50 mechanics. If my quarterly goal is to sell 100 wrenches, I can basically assume that I need to present them to about 340 mechanics. (30% success calling on 340 mechanics is 102 wrenches) If I'm working a full month of 20 days, I can further plan my month to ensure I present my wrenches to at least 17 mechanics per day in order to reach that 340 for the month. Breaking things down to simple, manageable, daily numbers helps large goals seem - and become - attainable. And if you really want to take it up a notch, figure out a way to increase that three out of ten to four or five. It is all about the numbers.

4 Your customer doesn't get it.

That's why you have a job. It can be frustrating to (feel like we) have the absolute best solution for the customer, yet they don't seem to understand or "get it." In other words, they don't see the fit as well as we do. On one hand, perhaps they need more education or information. On the other, they may be correct, that your product is not the best fit. Either way, it is up to YOU, the salesperson, to peel back the onion, determine the true reasons for buying (or not buying) and see if your product solves their problem. You can only do this if you truly understand their needs. Your need may not be their need. And only their need counts. It is up to you to find that need, help them fill it and solve their problem. If you cannot, or if it does not exist, it is time to move on.

5 Fill your brain with the good stuff.

Every day is a learning day, especially if you spend a lot of windshield time traveling from prospective client to prospective-client. What are you filling that time with? Jay-Z? Entertainment news? Top-notch sales professionals do as the legendary <u>Zig Ziglar</u> recommended, and turn their car into "automobile university." They listen to educational and motivational podcasts, books and programs. This strategy ensures that you are making daily deposits into the most important investment any professional has - himself! Don't be dismayed, however, and feel that your feel-good beats are gone forever. In his outstanding book <u>Psyched Up</u>, Daniel McGinn lays out the data, which shows that "feel-good" music can play a key role in preparing a salesperson to perform at their peak. Balance is key, and they each have their place.

*For more information about the people and books we highlight throughout this book, please visit **SaleSurgeBook.com**

6 Is a phone follow-up just as effective as an in-person visit?

The question could really be is anything - phone, email, fax - as effective as an in-person call. The answer is both no and yes. Generally speaking, an in-person visit is always the most effective, provided it is with the key decision-maker, because a large percentage of human communication is non-verbal. Hearing someone on the phone is one thing. Actually seeing, interacting and touching (appropriately of course!) is another thing entirely. Humans interact, communicate and bond much more effectively in person than via voice alone. Text and the written word is yet another step down in effective communication. That's not to say that they don't have a place, however. If there truly isn't any connection or reason for the prospect to move forward in communication with you, most any method of following up will yield the same result - nothing. Radio silence. And that is fine. It's time to move on. Sometimes it's wise to maximize your time and get to this point much more quickly and economically, by following up via phone rather than in-person.

7 Cure your aversion to cold calling.

Without sales, a business cannot grow or survive. Without sales professionals, most sales don't occur. Without prospects, sales professionals don't have anyone to sell to. So how do we find new, qualified sales prospects who have a need for what we sell? We search for them! Yes, that includes cold calling. It also includes other related methods of finding prospects, such as prospecting, hunting, farming and networking. Technically, cold calling refers to calls you make to prospects who don't know or trust you and who did not ask for your attention. It is you who are searching them out, initially to see if a need exists on their part. In most sales positions, cold calling is the key to growth, both for you and for your company, because it is theoretically a never-ending supply of possible sales. This should be exciting to you! There are plenty of books and resources to increase your comfort, and success, with cold calling. Just know that it can, and should, be a part of your sales job that you look forward to, because you never know what opportunities lie behind that next door you knock on. Curing any aversion to cold calling is a key to long-term sales growth and success.

8 Consistency is key.

There are a myriad of reasons why you cannot sell to your full potential today. Some are imagined, but many are real. Have you heard, or uttered, any of these?

The kids need to be picked up.
It is raining buckets.
The roads are covered in snow.
Today is a holiday.
The dog ate my proposal.
My company didn't send me enough pamphlets.
My customers don't want to see me on Fridays.
Nobody wants to buy anything in this lousy economy.
My car broke down.
I've faced such a string of rejection, I just need a day off.
My colleagues are on the beach, so why should I be out cold calling?

While many of these are legitimate barriers to the most effective selling, we need to keep the big picture in mind. Our overall mindset must be one of consistent activity, consistent improvement and consistent effort. This will unfailingly lead to consistent results. When the car breaks down, you prospect via phone and email. When the kids need to be picked up, you quickly stop in to visit that important client near their school. When some customers shut their doors on Friday, you search and find the ones that are open. You'll stand out and succeed. Consistently.

9 Kill the frog every day.

The legendary Brian Tracy often quotes Mark Twain, saying that if we do the most important, or most difficult, thing on our list first thing each day, everything else in our day will seem easy by comparison. We'll also have the satisfaction of knowing we succeeded in tackling our most important task. For many sales professionals, "eating the frog" is the term for cold calling or prospecting. As mentioned earlier, cold calling and prospecting are crucial to our continued growth and success. Therefore, we need to prioritize it consistently in our schedule. Doing the most important thing (Eating the frog) first ensures our success.

10 Get to know Brian Tracy.

Brian Tracy is one of the world's preeminent voices regarding sales success. His books, seminars, audio recordings and materials have helped millions of sales professionals learn and grow to reach the highest levels of sales achievement. You can certainly count me as a student of Brian Tracy, and the amount of success I've achieved because of his "mentorship" is incalculable. My personal favorite of his books is Advanced Selling Strategies, which is the most comprehensive book about professional selling I have ever read. The tips in this book are priceless and meant for the professional who is looking to build a long-term sales career. As I devoured this real-world collection of tips, principles and strategies, I was able to implement the tactics immediately. And best of all, these aren't fads or gimmick sales tricks to dupe or pressure customers. Tracy's thoughts and approach is all about helping us become better professionals so we may best serve our customers and build long-term, mutually beneficial relationships.

Truly a must read for any sales professional interested in growth and higher achievement.

*For more information about the people and books we highlight throughout this book, please visit **SaleSurgeBook.com**

11 How many referrals have you collected today?

A referral is, by far, the best lead you will have to sell your product or service. Think about it. Which scenario is more influential to your own behavior? A slick TV ad promoting the newest thriller movie, or your friend who tells you the movie was awesome? Of course, the friend's opinion had a far greater impact. It immediately put a favorable feeling about the movie into your head, and indicated that you had a high likelihood of feeling the same way. Your friend's referral lowered your guard and opened you up to give the movie some honest, sincere consideration. That is exactly what a business referral can do in sales. If Bruce refers you to Jim and says your services have been a great value added to his business, Jim will automatically expect that you can deliver the same results to him. The key is to exceed Bruce's expectations and, most importantly, ASK for the referral. Referrals turn cold calls into warm leads, but only when you ASK and receive them.

12 Busy does not equal successful.

The old 80/20 rule holds true in sales as much as in anything else. In other words, most of your results will come from 20% of your activity. Or from 20% of your customers. The big difference-maker is finding out what those key activities are and who those key customers are. Do you spend most of your time on those 20% activities, such as prospecting, meetings with qualified customers and relationship-building with existing customers? Or do you spend more time organizing your office, reviewing junk emails and filing papers? The key to short-term success, and long term growth, is to ensure that most of your time is spent with those crucial 20% activities that create the most tangible results.

13 Send the article.

A great way to build a network of strong friends and allies is to think of them constantly. Always consider the aspects of life that are important to them, and reach out to share things they'll find interesting and helpful. For example, if one of your best customers collects fine wine, and you read an interesting article about fine wine in a magazine or blog, clip it out and send it to your friend. He will be grateful for the information you shared and impressed that you thought of him. Plus, it is a great way to show you listen and are interested in your friend by giving, without any expectation of a return. You simple read something that would be of interest to him and shared it. So go ahead and send the article. It will show you truly care.

14 Send the note.

This is the Brian Buffini special. Buffini, one of the country's great business, real estate and self-development leaders, is known for his personal notes. He requires that his real estate coaching clients send personal notes every day, to build and solidify business and personal relationships. While most correspondence is not handled by text or email, a personal note will help you stand out above the crowd. It shows you spent some of your most valuable possession - your time - to craft a simple message to its recipient. This subtle, yet memorable, gesture is sure to propel you to the top of your customer's mind.

*For more information about the people and books we highlight throughout this book, please visit
SaleSurgeBook.com

15 Drop by.

This is another tactic perfected by Buffini and other real estate professionals, where a simple stop helps you greatly with relationship-building. A quick, unannounced stop with an encouraging word, small token of appreciation or item of value to the recipient can cement you as a thoughtful professional. Some real estate agents stop by with chocolate or calendars. The items doesn't matter as much as the message you are sending. I thought of you and you are important enough to me that I wanted to say a quick hello. One big caveat - some people, including this author, are not the biggest fans of unannounced stop-ins, depending on the scenario. A knock at the door when I've just stepped out of the shower is not the kind of drop-by I prefer. However, a business colleague making a quick pop-in would usually get a warm welcome. And I can't forget that real estate agent who dropped by and left some chocolate and a note on our front stoop many years ago. Her drop by helped her get the listing for the sale of our house and the purchase of our next home. Drop bys in the proper context are extremely effective.

16 What are your top five objections?

In any sales role, you are going to get hit with objections, or reasons people don't buy from you. After all, if there weren't any objections, you'd sell your product or service to every person you encountered. So if you know you are going to face these objections, it is crucial that you know how to combat them. And the first step in that process is to clearly identify what these objections are. Pick at least the top five objections you receive on a daily basis and craft simple, clear responses that can answer or disarm these objections. I should note that these must be truthful answers that explain why your product or service is in the best interest of your customer. And if it's not in their best interest, be honest and say that as well. If you know the top five objections that people have when they hear your presentation, you must be ready to answer the reasons you hear most frequently that they don't buy. Better yet, address these objections during your initial sales presentation, in an effort to completely take them off the table. For example, I once sold a product that many customers said was highly priced. The truth, however, was that my product cost less than the competitors when you looked at the cost of ownership over time. As such, I included early in my presentation the cost of owning the competing products. I laid out what they did and how much they cost to use over time. Then, when I came to the cost of my product, it was much less in comparison. I was simply helping the customer see the whole picture and put my product in perspective relative to the others, since that was a common objective I'd heard often. As a result, many customers now saw my product as the more cost-effective option it was. Only by clearly defining this objection was I able to proactively answer this concern for the customer.

17 What did you learn about your industry today?

Make a commitment to yourself - to know a little more and be a little better each day. Can you learn a new fact about a competitor? A new way of communicating? A simple habit to boost productivity? Are there new trends that complement your product or service? You never know when these topics may help, or when they will come up in conversation with a customer. The more you learn about your industry, the better prepared you will be to stand out as an expert and trusted partner.

18 Tops in sales does not necessarily equal tops in management.

Far too often we see top-producing sales professionals promoted into management, only to bomb out and hurt the organization. Why? The main reason is that the skills required to become and remain a top-producing sales rep are often not the same as the skills required to become a leader, manager and coach of sales reps. While high-level success should be a prerequisite for leadership positions, there are a plethora of additional skills required to lead effectively. Communicating and motivating a team is entirely than managing a customer base. Not that one is better than the other, but they each require a unique set of related skills, abilities and aptitudes. Sometimes the top-producing sales professional is best suited to remain as such.

19 Align with the company culture.

This one decision will have a large part to do with your long-term happiness with the sales organization. Are they hard-charging and ruthless? Do they value integrity, family and teamwork? These are just a few of the factors that create the culture of a sales organization, and it is wise to understand these fully before you join the team. Many of us have been in situations where we are interviewing for a sales position but, ultimately, come to a point where we know it just won't be a good cultural fit. For me, it was when a potential sales manager said, "We want someone in this position who will see the job as their life. They will live, eat and breathe this job. To succeed, it must be all-consuming in your life." We parted ways amicably, knowing that this particular culture didn't fit what I was looking for. Aligning with company culture is crucial to long-term success and happiness.

20 Organize your bag.

You must know exactly what resources you have and where to find them at a moment's notice. When you customer asks a pointed question - one that you have resources or materials to help explain - you need to be ready to professionally turn to those resources. It may be a white paper, a price list, a product information guide, a package insert, a product manual, an industry publication, etc. Know what resources you have, and where to find them quickly to help educate your customer.

21 Set boundaries on your time.

What are the "must-do" items for your day? What items can wait? Make a point to prioritize your activities so you achieve the most important tasks, while also working toward those further down the list. For example, if you have an hour blocked for a customer meeting prior to a must-do activity, make it a point to hold yourself to that schedule. Setting boundaries and limits on your time will ensure that you stay focused and complete the most important tasks in your day. It will also show your customers that you value your time, as well as theirs. And the more they sense you valuing your time, the more they will value it as well.

22 The customer is always right.

Sometimes they are wrong, but they are right. Sometimes they are irrational, but they are right. Sometimes they are unrealistic, but they are right. No sale occurs without a customer, and to the degree you can, our job is to maintain the relationship and move toward a mutually-beneficial outcome. I'd rather win a sale than an argument.

23 Get to know Zig Ziglar.

He was possibly the most well-known self-help and sales leadership coaching expert we have ever known. A stickler for a customer-centered, ethical sales approach, Ziglar was fond of saying, "Help enough people get what they want and you'll get what you want." He was the author of many sales and leadership classics, including See You at the Top and Born to Win. If you need a mentor to start your sales career, start with the legend, Zig Ziglar.

*For more information about the people and books we highlight throughout this book, please visit **SaleSurgeBook.com**

24 In ten seconds, what do you sell?

You must be crystal clear about what it is your product or service provides, and be able to get that point across without thinking. Some call it an "elevator pitch." In other words, can you verbalize your value in the time it takes to get on and off an elevator. This must be ingrained and natural, so it flows off your tongue in an instant. This will allow you to work off of this value proposition in any selling conversation you may find yourself engaged in.

25 Set one, three and five-year goals.

Sales professionals tend to be goal-driven beings. We do our best when we have a clear idea of what we want to achieve, and when we need to achieve it. Remember, a goal without a deadline is just a wish. Choosing short term goals as soon as one year, and longer-term goals for three, five and more years allow us to experience the satisfaction of achievement while aiming still toward something greater. As the previously-mentioned Zig Ziglar used to say, "If you aim at nothing, you'll hit it every time." Goals give us direction and purpose.

26 What podcasts have you listened to today?

In the good old days, self-improvement consisted of wearing out cassette tapes of greats like Zig Ziglar, Earl Nightingale and Jim Rohn. Occasionally, the tapes would break and require repair using scotch tape and a great deal of manual dexterity. These days, however, it is much more efficient and cost-effective to learn from others in any area of focus. Thankfully, smart phones and podcasts have replaced cassette tapes and compact disks. We can literally listen to anyone talk about anything, wherever we are! Talk about a traveling university! Take advantage and use technology to improve every day.

*For more bonus information about the awesome books, influential thought leaders and helpful links we refer to in the book, please visit:
SaleSurgeBook.com

27 Get to know Earl Nightingale.

His classic audio recording, "The Strangest Secret," put forth the assertion that our thoughts ultimately control our actions and our success. He was a great forerunner for many future self-help gurus, many of whom were raised listening to Earl Nightingale's booming voice and powerful insight.

*For more bonus information about the awesome books, influential thought leaders and helpful links we refer to in the book, please visit:
SaleSurgeBook.com

28 Executives are busy.

Don't waste their time, ever. The first time you waste a busy executive's time will be the last time you get the chance to do so. Always have a reason and purpose for them to see you. Give them some value and leave them pleased that they took a minute to see you. You won't always have the opportunity to close the sale, but many times you'll have a chance to advance the sale. Strive to bring value and give a busy professional a reason to interact with you.

29 What happens two minutes after you leave?

What will they say about you, your product or your visit? Will they snicker as you walk away? Will they shake their head and treat you like any other salesperson? Or will they say to one another, "that guy really cares about us and our problems. And he always helps us!" Make a positive impact that will shape their future thoughts about you and your company.

30 What is your brand?

No, I don't mean your company. And I don't mean your product. I mean, your brand. It is the feeling and impression that sticks with people regarding you and your offerings. Your brand may include the fact that you always follow up, or that you always dress professionally, or that you always tell jokes. The biggest factor in building your brand is YOU, and it transcends what you sell or who you work for.

31 Do you make the team better?

Sports metaphors are often over-used when talking about sales and business, although team players may be an exception. They are always welcome, wherever they work and whatever they do. Team players do more than just follow the rules. They help others achieve more and reach greater heights. It may be through a simple word of encouragement, a helpful tip or a piece of competitive insight. These players become far more valuable than their stats, or sales numbers, indicate. Are you a team player that makes the team better?

32 Don't gamble on your future.

Never risk tomorrow by engaging in questionable sales behavior today. Unethical, illegal or shady dealings will always come back to bite you eventually. They are not worth the risk. You'll be better off falling short of your sales goals today, rather than going below the line to hit the number.

33 The industry and you.

Is it a fit? Knowing your strengths and weaknesses will help you pinpoint industries where you will most likely succeed or fail. For example, if you are a highly technical, detail-oriented person, you may achieve great things selling computer hardware or software. You may not excel at a more relational sale, such as selling advertising time. Not that analytical smarts or relational skills won't translate across industries - they certainly will - but you will scale your highest mountains in areas that are the best match for your skills, abilities and interests.

34 (First-rate) recruiters can be your ally.

Searching for sales positions can be great in that you can "hire" recruiters to search with, and for, you. They succeed, and get paid, if and only if you are hired. Let them tap into their networks to search for opportunities that match your skills, abilities and interests. However, like sales professionals, all recruiters are not created the same. Some will tell you what you want to hear and fill you with pie-in-the-sky predictions - "I will find you your dream job in 30 days,".... "I will help you double your income, no question about it,".... "I am filling dozens of new positions every week."

However, real, successful, proven recruiters will help you find your next position, by fitting your experience with the right opportunity. And the good recruiters will also share their honest opinions about your strengths and perceived weaknesses from the perspective of employers. Use solid recruiters and build relationships with them. They are often a big difference-maker in helping you find your next great sales opportunity.

35 Don't neglect your family.

There is no job on the planet worth ruining your family. If you have kids, try always to realize they will only be young once. 12-hour days and nights on the road are okay on occasion, or during a season of your working life, but they should never become the norm. That is, if you have a family that is a high priority in your life. When you are are work - work. And when you are home with the kids during off-hours - be with THEM. As hard-charging, goal-oriented professionals that get things done, we all need a reminder from time to time. And my reminder is...right now. I'm going to go put the kids to bed.

36 Video vs text.

Which is better at connecting with your potential customers? This is debatable and varies, in large degree, based on your industry. For example, many younger professionals in the technology space prefer short video emails rather than text. Due, in large part, to social media, this is how millennial hipsters have been raised and trained to consume information. Professionals in more mature industries like finance, for example, might prefer a more black-and-white, traditional email with easy-to-understand sentences and paragraphs. Different audiences, different methods of communication. They each have their place, and it is our job as professionals to know which resonates better with our customers and prospects.

37 Don't bad-mouth the competition.

Talking bad about the other guy always makes you look small. If they are inferior, you come across as lowering yourself to that level. If they are better, you seem envious and petty. Either way, bad-mouthing a competitor shows a lack of confidence on your part. Be proud of your product or service, and certainly point of the benefits and advantages you have over your competition. This is done best in the spirit of educating your customer, such as, "A couple of the things you'll love about our model over the other brands are our warranty and high-powered engine." These are factual points of distinction that may help your customer make an informed decision. And to show real confidence, point out a strength your competition may have over YOU. This is how you transform - in your customer's eyes - from salesperson to valued consultant.

38 Dress as if you were a professional.

The first impression you make with a potential customer sends a message - one that is either positive or negative. Simply looking like a well-groomed, well-dressed professional gives others a sense of confidence about you. They can sense you are a person of authority, even if they have never heard you speak a word. In addition, you should dress to the culture of your customer. For example, don't show up trying to sell farm equipment on a ranch wearing a three-piece suit. Dress for the clientele. If you are calling on executives or medical professionals, that suit would work quite nicely.

Many years ago, a sage professional athlete had it right when he said, "If I look good, I feel good. If I feel good, I play good. If I play good, they pay good." Deion Sanders had it right, for us sales professionals too.

39 Identify the culture of the customer.

If they wear overalls, don't show up in a tux. If they work evenings and weekends, the best way of connecting will be to show up during those times. Whenever possible, meet them on their terms in their comfort zone. Is their culture extremely formal regarding dress, language and behavior? In this case, you wouldn't want to speak in a bodacious, slang-filled, attention-grabbing manner. You'd never want to stray from your own personal values, and sometimes their culture simply won't be a fit for you. Wherever possible, however, do what you can to fit in as one with your customer's culture.

40 Objections are not personal.

We all make decisions - business or personal - based on a simple value proposition. Is what I can purchase more valuable than the amount of money I'd have to give up to acquire the item or service? That is the basic question. As Tony Robbins puts it, am I being driven by the pain of my situation or the pleasure the product or service would provide, and are either of these stimuli strong enough to force me to change my behavior? These are reasons we purchase goods and services, or make decisions to change our behavior, as Robbins has led millions to do over the years. Objections are not personal, they are the result of a simple, personal value proposition that is unique to each and every prospect. As a professional, you cannot become offended when a customer decides not to purchase from you today, or ever. In most cases, it has much more to do with them than it does with you.

41 Know your "WHY."

This one tip with help you get through the tough times and stay focused on the finish line. Why are you involved in this endeavor? Why are you getting up every morning to do what you do? Is it for personal satisfaction? For your family? To set up a comfortable retirement? To achieve financial independence? To put a child through a pricey, private university? Whatever your personal driving force, you must keep in top of mind as a reminder of the end result. Simon Sinek wrote the book about finding your why, and it remains a true classic for anyone interested in personal or professional growth. This WHY is the goal that will pull you through when you feel like calling it a day but, instead, make one final call on a prospect. This will help you get out there to make it happen when it's 10 degrees outside and you feel like lingering in bed. Your why is your why, and nobody else's. It is important and deeply personal, acting as the driving force behind every move you make.

42 Know your customer's "WHY."

Just as you have a WHY, so does your customer. The moment your product or service allows them to get closer to that WHY, he will buy from you. Dig deep to find the true motivation behind your customer's buying decisions. Does your product line up with those values and help him get closer to the big WHY? If not, perhaps he's not the right prospect. If so, you can create a win/win and deliver value that delights your customer.

43 Track expenses.

Whether you work for a large corporation or as a sole proprietor, you'll always need to understand where you are spending your money. This will allow you to not only be prepared for tax time, but you'll also be able to assess whether your resources are being devoted to worthwhile clients or campaigns. In other words, are you seeing a return on your investment? Are there any specific investments that do or do not yield a short or long-term result? If you find certain spending activities are documented to be profitable, perhaps you should build on them. If others provide no ROI (return-on-investment), consider cutting them out. Similar to a budget for tracking personal, household expenses, a professional or sales budget will help you track your expenses and allow you to become more efficient and profitable.

44 Manage the adrenaline.

Try not to ride the emotional roller coaster of sales. Never get too high or too low. When times are good, enjoy them, but realize that a career in sales usually runs in cycles. Some days, months or years are great, while others are lackluster. Try to avoid getting super-high or terribly low. Ride the ups and downs with a consistent, positive approach. A good rule of thumb is - you are not as good as you feel on your best days, and never as bad as you feel on your lowest. When you land that big deal, celebrate without getting cocky or arrogant. Remind yourself that bad days are inevitable. When times are tough, remember that better days, and more sales, are waiting around the corner. Recall the high points in your career when everything went your way. Consistency in effort and attitude is a crucial key to long-term sales success.

45 Attack today while thinking long-term.

As sales professionals, we must always take care of today's duties while planning for tomorrow's opportunities. The key is strong, deliberate long-term planning. Just as we felt the pinch if we waited until the night before the 3rd grade social studies final exam to finally crack a book and study, we'll feel that same pressure as a sales professional. Sometimes things need to be done and obstacles must be tackled, today. Other strategic items can be planned for and executed upon gradually, or when the future time arises. What we cannot do, however, is chase our tail constantly by putting out today's fires while paying no mind to the opportunities, challenges and imperatives of tomorrow. Balance and preparation are crucial.

46 A sale today is not worth damaging your reputation.

If you've been in sales longer than a week, you've probably encountered a situation where you could go for a big win today, while at the same time creating some future animosity toward you or your company. For example, you know your company is about to offer a large discount for the purchase of your big piece of equipment, however you have the opportunity to sell it today, at a higher commission rate, to a loyal customer. Should you take the bigger payday today, even though your customer will find out you cost them an opportunity for savings? The answer came directly from the mouth of Jesus, more than 2000 years ago during his Sermon on the Mount. He said, "Do unto others as you would have them do unto you." In other words, put yourself in your customer's shoes. What would you prefer to have done unto you? Of course, you would want to know about the upcoming special so you could decide what is best for your long-term business interests. And after all, if this is a "loyal" customer, they've more than earned this treatment. Plus, it is good business that will come back to help you in the long-run. They will appreciate your consideration, and you'll come across as an ally, rather than a slick salesperson.

47 Get to know Napoleon Hill.

Hill's classic book about personal achievement and attaining true riches, Think and Grow Rich, is a must-read for anyone searching for higher levels of success. Hill learned under the great Andrew Carnegie and countless others, and from these great giants of personal achievement, developed a common philosophy that formed the foundation of their greatness. That formula is available to us today, for those who wish to apply its principles toward a successful sales career.

*For more bonus information about the awesome books, influential thought leaders and helpful links we refer to in the book, please visit:
SaleSurgeBook.com

48 The supermarket duck-away.

When you see that kinda-sorta friend at the supermarket, how do you approach them? If you are like most people, you either go forward to offer a hearty, sincere greeting…..or you do the duck away. You know how that goes….you're scanning the aisle for your prefered type of salad dressing, until you see that acquaintance of yours. Immediately, you ditch the dressing and head for the meats. You are outta that aisle as fast and smoothly as can be, regardless of the condiments you're leaving behind. This is the classic duck-away, and often it stems from a feeling deep down that you aren't living up to your potential. You are in a season of life you are less-than-proud of, and you don't really want to talk about it with anyone. For many of us, this feel stems from dissatisfaction in either a career, relationship or lack thereof. For sales professionals, you can learn a lot from your propensity to do the duck-away. This could be a red flag, telling you as clear as day that your chosen company, product or, even, career path are not a good fit for you.

Are you selling a product you don't truly believe it? Are you proud to tell friends and family what you sell? Are you working with people who don't share your values, and who you really don't want to be connected to? These are questions sales professionals need to ask themselves regularly, especially if you find your supermarket duck-aways increasing.

49 Don't be cute with your customer.

Don't patronize them. Don't try to trick them. Don't talk down to them. Don't lead them down a path to meet your goals. In other words, treat them like real people whom you care for professionally. Do what's best for them. Treat them the way you'd like to be treated. Be honest and fair. Go the extra mile whenever it is to their benefit. Take the blame when mistakes are made. Then, if you do all of this and they still don't value you, trust you or buy from you - fire them. Walk away and find a customer who will appreciate these wonderful traits on your end and partner with you to build a mutually-beneficial business relationship.

50 With multiple products, what is most important to the customer?

Whenever possible, tailor your presentations and offerings to the needs of your customer. Sales professionals are often pressured by management to sell the highest priced products first, only then falling back on the lower-profit offerings. What this often does, however, is create immediate friction over a lack of sale, making the second product more difficult to sell. In other words, you are creating a NO before you get to the most appropriate YES. For example, you go to the pool store to purchase a new filter for your pool, and the sales rep spends 20 minutes trying to upsell you to a brand new pool. Instead, as a sales professional, go right for the product that most effectively meets their wants, needs and desires. In other words, they want a pool filter, sell them a pool filter. You'll get the sale and they'll be delighted. This, now, is the exact frame of mind and foundation on which to build toward your biggest and most important sale. And if they have a need, they are already comfortable enough to buy from you. You can casually ask if they've noticed the beautiful new pools in the showroom. You've warmed up the relationship and built trust. In fact, because you began the relationship focusing on their needs, they are now in a position to look at your other products, even when they never intended to from the start. You focused on them and earned the chance.

The next step…

If you enjoyed Sales Surge, you may also like the 2nd book…..

Sales Surge Sequel: Another 50 Secrets to Boost Your Sales Career With Less Stress and More Fun!

Available on Amazon and Audible

*For more bonus information about the awesome books, influential thought leaders and helpful links we refer to in the book, please visit:
SaleSurgeBook.com

We hope these tips will help you supercharge your career, so you enjoy the sales surge you are looking for.

Thanks for reading!

www.ingramcontent.com/pod-product-compliance
Lightning Source LLC
Chambersburg PA
CBHW030727180526
45157CB00008BA/3076